Who Were Stanley and Livingstone?

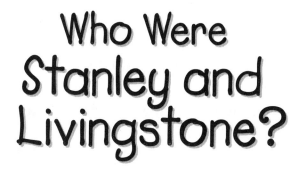

by Jim Gigliotti

illustrated by David Malan

Penguin Workshop

For Sophia: world traveler,
explorer of distant lands—JG

To Emmett, keep exploring—DM

PENGUIN WORKSHOP
An imprint of Penguin Random House LLC, New York

First published in the United States of America by Penguin Workshop,
an imprint of Penguin Random House LLC, New York, 2021

Text copyright © 2021 by Jim E. Gigliotti
Illustrations copyright © 2021 by Penguin Random House LLC

PENGUIN is a registered trademark and PENGUIN WORKSHOP is a trademark
of Penguin Books Ltd. WHO HQ & Design is a registered trademark
of Penguin Random House LLC.

Visit us online at penguinrandomhouse.com.

Library of Congress Control Number: 2021020894

Printed in the United States of America

ISBN 9780399544194 (paperback)   10 9 8 7 6 5 4 3 2 1 WOR
ISBN 9780399544217 (library binding)   10 9 8 7 6 5 4 3 2 1 WOR

Contents

Who Were Stanley and Livingstone?

One day in 1871, a man hobbled from his hut in a small village in East Africa to see what all the excitement outside was about. He was only fifty-eight, but his gray beard and rough skin, worn and wrinkled from many years of working outdoors in harsh conditions, made him look much older. He moved slowly, too, because he had been sick for a very long time. To the people in the village of Ujiji, he was almost a member of their family. To the rest of the world, he was the famous Scottish explorer Dr. David Livingstone. But the rest of the world had not seen Dr. Livingstone in more than five years. Most people assumed that he was probably dead.

The excitement was created by the arrival of a younger man who had brought dozens of people with him—native Africans who helped him on his journey. They carried enough supplies to last for years. They blew their horns and waved an American flag. The younger man was Henry Morton Stanley, a thirty-year-old journalist who had traveled to Africa to search for Dr. Livingstone. Stanley, and all the people who read his newspaper articles, wanted to know for sure if Dr. Livingstone was dead or alive.

Stanley walked forward, took off his helmet, and reached his hand toward the older man.

"Dr. Livingstone, I presume?" he asked.

Of course it was Dr. Livingstone! They were the only two European men present. But Stanley couldn't think of anything else to say. He was nervous. At the time, Dr. Livingstone was one of the most famous people in the world. Stanley wanted Livingstone to like him.

He had traveled for nearly eight months into the middle of the African continent looking for Livingstone. But he never imagined what he might say if he ever found him. So he said the first thing that came to his mind: a very proper greeting.

Stanley didn't need to be nervous. Dr. Livingstone was happy to see him. The older man needed the medicine and supplies that Stanley had carried with him or he wouldn't live much longer.

Over the next several months, the two men became good friends. They enjoyed long talks about many subjects. After Dr. Livingstone got better, the two men even explored parts of Africa together.

And then Henry Morton Stanley left Africa. The two men were together for just over four months. But they have been linked ever since. It's almost as if "Stanley and Livingstone" was one name.

But who was Stanley? And who was Livingstone? Did they ever see each other again? Why are they such important figures in world history? And why did "Dr. Livingstone, I presume?" become such a famous line? Let's explore their story!

CHAPTER 1
Young Livingstone

As a child, David Livingstone shared a single room with his family in an apartment house in Blantyre, Scotland, a country in the United Kingdom, which also includes England, Wales, and Northern Ireland.

It wasn't too crowded in that room when David was born on March 19, 1813—just him, his mother, Agnes, his father, Neil, and his brother, John, who was almost two years older. Over the next several years, though, Agnes and Neil had several more children—two girls and another boy —and it became very crowded! Two other children died when they were still babies.

The entire family did everything in their one room. They cooked, ate, cleaned, studied, and slept there. There was enough room for the beds because they fit underneath each other—smaller ones on wheels tucked under larger ones. At night, the family rolled out the beds, which took up much of the space in the room.

The Livingstones' room was one of eight on their floor of the building. One family lived in each of the eight rooms. And the building had three floors. So twenty-four families lived in the building!

Some of the families kept chickens or other animals in their rooms, even though it was against the rules. All of them threw their garbage down holes cut into the building's staircases. And all of them used an old-fashioned toilet that was simply a pail they kept covered with dirt.

The building smelled. It was dirty. And there were far too many people living there. David did not have a comfortable life while growing up.

David's father traveled door-to-door selling tea. But most of the families in the building had someone who worked in the local cotton mill, where yarn and cloth were made. The owner of the cotton mill made a lot of money and lived in a big house in the town. But he paid his workers very little.

Neil Livingstone didn't have a job at the mill, but he didn't make very much money selling tea, either. So the boys of the Livingstone family went to work in the cotton mill when they were still children.

David was just ten when he began his first job at the mill as a piecer. Working as a piecer meant fixing the threads that broke on the spinning machines. Piecers were often children because the job meant crawling under machinery or climbing on top of it. They were better at this than adults,

and their size was more suited to the job, which was hard, dangerous work!

The hours at the mill were long and the building was hot. Mill workers, including the children, worked from six o'clock in the morning until eight at night. The mill was almost ninety degrees inside because the heat was good for the cotton. Sometimes the piecers had a bucket of water poured over them. It wasn't to cool off, though. It was to wake them up if they were getting tired near the end of a long day. Still, that was better than the other punishment they received if they didn't spot threads that broke: a beating with a leather strap.

By the end of the day, many of the piecers were too tired to do anything but go home and sleep so they could do it all again the next day. Not David, though. After he got off work, he went to an evening school. Lessons were taught for two hours beginning at eight o'clock at night.

The teacher was a man hired by the mill. Then, after David was done at ten o'clock, he went home to read. Often, he read books about science and geography. He read until at least midnight, and sometimes later. Then his mother would take the book out of his hands and tell him to sleep. After all, he had to be back at work again by six o'clock in the morning! It was a tough life, but David wasn't unhappy.

The first time David got paid, most of what he earned went straight to his parents. But with the little bit left over, he bought a book to learn Latin. When David wasn't studying Latin, he especially liked to read books on travel. He dreamed of seeing the world outside Scotland and of visiting the places he read about. They were far, far away from the cotton mill of Blantyre.

David's father, however, wanted him to read books about religion. The Livingstones were Christian. Neil didn't like it when David read books about science. He thought that sometimes science tried to take the place of God.

Every Sunday, the family walked more than two miles to the town of Hamilton to attend church.

David agreed with his father about Christianity, but he disagreed with him about science. David looked around at the beauty of nature and felt as if science proved that there is a God.

When David was in his late teens, he became a spinner in the mill. That was a more important job. It also meant that he wasn't always standing, like the piecers did. It allowed him to read even while he was at the mill. He would set a book on his machine and read while he worked.

The cotton mill was a noisy place. There were many people moving around. The frames of the machines clanged together. Iron wheels moved back and forth on iron rails. But David learned to focus even with all the noise.

One day, David's father brought home a paper about medical missionaries in China. Missionaries are people who travel to another country to teach about their religion. Medical missionaries also help take care of the sick. David thought it could be a great way for him to help other people. He was very interested in science, so becoming a doctor made sense. And he wanted to travel, so becoming a missionary was a perfect fit.

It cost money to go to medical school, of course. But because David was now a spinner, he was getting paid more. He managed to save some of his salary for school. And in 1836, when he was twenty-three, he began studying at Anderson's College in Glasgow, Scotland.

In 1840, David qualified as both a doctor and a missionary. He had joined the London Missionary Society, which sent people all over the world to teach about Christianity.

David previously had wanted to go to China, but he was ultimately sent to join a mission in Africa. He sailed from London, England, on December 8, 1840.

CHAPTER 2
Young Stanley

Henry Morton Stanley was an American journalist. But there was a lot about his life that wasn't quite what it seemed. For instance, Henry Morton Stanley wasn't even his real name! He hadn't been born in America, either. And he had not been a journalist for much of his life. In fact, he made up so many details about himself that it is sometimes difficult for historians to know what is true and what is not.

Stanley's real name was John Rowlands, and he was born in Denbigh (say: DEN-bee), Wales, in the United Kingdom on January 28, 1841.

Like David Livingstone, John was very poor while growing up. But unlike David, John was not always part of a loving family. He never knew his father, and his mother, Elizabeth Parry, sent him to live with his grandfather when he was just a baby.

Denbigh, Wales

John's grandfather, who was named Moses and who also lived in Denbigh, took good care of him. John liked Moses. The two of them went everywhere together. But when John was five years old, his grandfather died suddenly. Now where would he go?

Two of John's uncles lived nearby and were making a good living. They paid a local family to take care of the boy.

But the arrangement didn't last very long.

The family took care of John for only about six months when his uncles stopped paying them. The family had four children of their own. They couldn't take care of another child for free. So one morning in 1847, when John was only six, he was brought to a workhouse and left there. It was John's new home.

St. Asaph Workhouse, Denbigh, Wales

In nineteenth-century Wales, a workhouse was a place where very poor people—adults, children, and sometimes even entire families—could get food and shelter.

In return for meals and a place to live, anyone who was healthy enough worked during the day.

Young John did not like the workhouse at all, as some of the conditions were grim. But some good did come from living there. John received an education. He learned to write and to do arithmetic. Mostly, he learned to read—and he read a lot! "I became infected with a passion for books," he once said. Reading was the way he escaped his harsh daily life. He read anything he could get his hands on.

However, in the workhouse, he was mostly limited to religious books.

When John left the workhouse, it was to begin training as a teacher. Over the next two years, he lived with relatives in several different cities, but had trouble finding a job. In 1858, he worked for a butcher in Liverpool, one of the largest and most crowded cities in England. A butcher is a person who sells meat.

One day in late December 1858, seventeen-year-old John delivered an order of meat to a ship that was going to bring cloth from Liverpool to the United States. The captain suggested that John join the crew. He promised John five dollars a month and new clothes to come aboard

as his personal cabin boy. Being a cabin boy meant delivering messages from the captain, looking out for other ships or obstacles, and maybe even steering the ship if the sea was calm. It often led to more responsibility on the next voyage.

But the captain tricked John. Instead of being a cabin boy, he was sent to work below the deck. It was the roughest, dirtiest, hardest job on board. The captain figured that John would run off when the boat reached the United States. Then the captain wouldn't have to pay him! And his plan worked.

After the ship reached New Orleans, Louisiana, in February 1859, John left without telling anybody. He didn't have any money, but at least

he was free of his life aboard ship. He was a confident young man and believed he could find work on his own.

It didn't take long. The way John told the story, he was roaming the streets of New Orleans during his first week in the city when he came across a wealthy-looking man. John approached him and confidently asked if he might be looking to hire someone. Sure enough, the man bought and sold cotton, the major crop in the American South. He always had work to be done, and he liked John's attitude. So he hired the teenager.

Soon, the businessman became more like a father than a boss to John. The older man taught John about his business. They read great books together. John said the older man even adopted him, although he may have made up that story. Still, John said, the older man meant so much to him that the teenager decided to take his name:

Henry Stanley. John began calling himself Henry
Stanley, too. He added the middle name Morton
later.

CHAPTER 3
Into Africa

Less than two months after John Rowlands was born, Dr. David Livingstone arrived in Cape Town, South Africa, in March 1841. It was just before his twenty-eighth birthday.

At this time, the interior of Africa was largely unknown to the world outside of anyone living there. The continent spans five thousand miles from north to south and is nearly the same distance across, from east to west. This vast expanse of land includes deserts, savannas, dense jungles, rivers, and lakes.

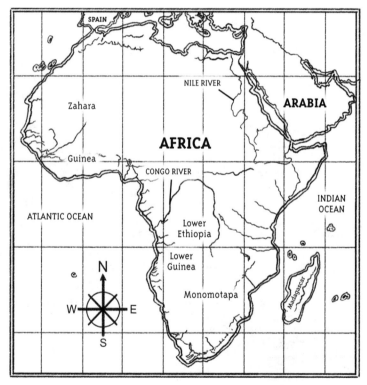

Nineteenth-century map of Africa

The rest of the world knew about its coastal boundaries and seaports because African goods such as gold, salt, and beads had been traded for European goods such as rum, iron, and guns for hundreds of years. The dreadful practice of shipping enslaved people across the Atlantic Ocean was also launched from those seaports. But much of the middle of the African continent was a mystery to outsiders.

Before leaving England, Livingstone had learned to speak Dutch because the Netherlands had been trading with coastal cities in Africa for a very long time and some Dutch merchants lived there. He learned Setswana, a language spoken by millions of Africans. He also learned important skills such as navigation. That is, using instruments and objects such as the stars to figure out where you are and how to get where you are going.

Octant (navigational tool)

Livingstone traveled north from Cape Town to the village of Kuruman. Robert Moffat, a

Robert Moffat

missionary he had met in London, already lived there. David was excited. He couldn't wait to get going. He was determined to make Christianity as important to the native people of South Africa as it was to him.

But Livingstone found that Moffat had convinced very few Africans at Kuruman to become Christians. Livingstone believed it would be better for him to start his own mission and do things his own way. So he continued north, about five hundred miles, to set up a mission at Mabotsa. It was his first trip into the African interior.

Livingstone battled the intense heat, fierce winds, monsoon rains—and more. Worst of all for him was a lion attack at Mabotsa in 1844.

Several lions had been killing the villagers' cows and sheep there. Livingstone and some men from the village tried to scare them off. But when one lion was shot, he attacked Livingstone, springing at him and closing his huge mouth around the missionary's left arm. "Growling horribly close to my ear, he shook me as a terrier dog does a rat," Livingstone said.

The lion let go only when Livingstone's assistant shot at it. Livingstone had several teeth marks on his arm and a broken bone that never fully healed properly.

Still, he never panicked during the attack. Instead, he said, he was thinking about "which part of me the brute would eat first." Afterward, he realized he had come close to death but was not afraid.

The attack forced Livingstone to return to Kuruman to recover. There, he once again met with Robert Moffat, who now had his daughter, Mary, with him. Livingstone and Mary became

engaged. In 1845, they were married. The next year, they had a son, Robert. He was the first of three boys and three girls in their family.

Over the next several years, Livingstone and his

Mary Moffat

growing family traveled from mission to mission in Africa. He had little success. Livingstone usually looked on the bright side of things. But he was frustrated at not being able to convince people, including those in the Bakgatla and Koena tribes, to become Christians. Still, he was more frustrated with something else: slavery.

Beginning in the fifteenth century, several European countries sought to increase their national wealth through the slave trade.

People were captured and enslaved by African tribes that attacked other tribes, or by European or Arab raiders. Many of these enslaved people were sent to the Americas. In turn, the Americas sent raw goods such as cotton, sugar, and tobacco to European nations. And European nations sent guns and other factory-made goods to Africa. This three-sided arrangement resulted in more than twelve million enslaved people being shipped from the coasts of Africa over a period of about four hundred years. The number could even be higher because many died on the journey due to violence and horrible conditions on the ships.

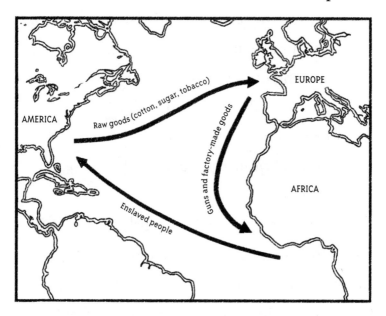

The triangular route of the Atlantic slave trade

In 1807, the United States had made it illegal to import any enslaved people from Africa. In 1833, England passed an act to end slavery everywhere its empire ruled. But in Africa, Arab and Portuguese merchants still traded goods for people they had captured. Livingstone was shocked to see the horrible treatment of enslaved people by both outsiders and fellow Africans. He came to believe the best way to end slavery was to convince tribal leaders to grow their own goods such as cotton and sugar, and then find a way for them to ship goods from the interior of the continent to the seaports. That way they could trade those goods for what they needed instead of trading human beings.

But Livingstone knew that the only way they could do that was by finding a waterway that went all the way to the sea. So beginning in 1849, David Livingstone began to search for one. He started spending less time as a missionary and more time as an explorer.

In 1852, Mary and the children returned to the United Kingdom. The next year, David began a trip from the interior of the African continent westward to the Atlantic Ocean. Then

David and Mary Livingstone with four of their six children

he reversed direction and headed back, all the way to the Indian Ocean. He traveled more than four thousand miles in all. As usual, he hired a group of local men to help guide him, carry supplies, and offer protection.

He encountered many difficulties that explorers faced. One time, a group of angry villagers near Manyuema chucked deadly spears at him and his men. Another time, a hippopotamus dove underneath his boat, then rose up, toppling it over!

He fought malaria and other diseases. But in May 1854, he reached the Atlantic Ocean at Luanda, on the west coast of southern Africa. Two years later, in May 1856, he reached the Indian Ocean at Quelimane in Mozambique. It had taken him almost four years to make the entire journey.

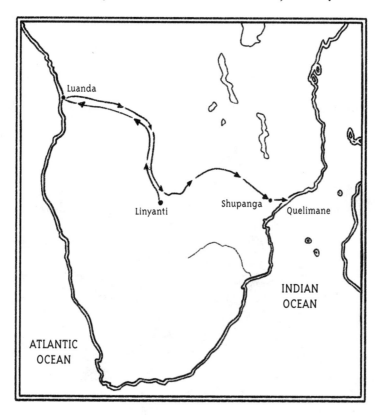

Livingstone's route across the continent of Africa, 1853–1856

Victoria Falls

Along the way, in November 1855, Livingstone became the first European to see the thunderous waterfall on the Zambezi River that the people of southern Africa called Mosi-oa-Tunya, which means "The Smoke that Thunders." Livingstone named it "Victoria Falls," after England's Queen Victoria. He was also the first European to ever cross the African continent. This was big news!

Queen Victoria (1819–1901)

Princess Alexandrina Victoria was only eighteen years old in 1837 when her uncle, King William IV, died. As the next in line to the throne, Victoria became queen of the United Kingdom. She ruled until her death almost sixty-four years later.

Her time as queen was a period of great growth in the United Kingdom. There were many advances in science, engineering, and medicine. And through trade and manufacturing, the country became very wealthy. It grew to include many territories, called colonies, around the world. Colonies are nations or groups of people governed by a different country. They are usually established for the economic good of the governing country, not always to the benefit of the people being governed.

During Victoria's reign, these colonies, called the British Empire, were all over the world. Eventually, it became the largest empire in the history of the world.

The period from about 1820–1914 has come to be known as the Victorian era.

While traveling, Livingstone kept extensive journals about his explorations. He also wrote many letters to friends and colleagues. He kept 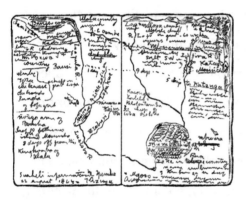 them all in a watertight box. He would give the letters to merchants or slave traders on their way east. They delivered them to Zanzibar, a small island off the east coast of Africa that had a British government office. From there, they were sent to England. It wasn't a perfect system—sometimes Livingstone's letters took more than a year to reach home! But they allowed British newspapers to report on each new discovery. By the time Livingstone completed his coast-to-coast journey, he had become a national hero. London's Royal Geographical Society (RGS) awarded him a gold medal for "the encouragement and promotion of geographical science and discovery" and a cash prize, even though he wasn't there to accept them.

Finally, in December 1856, Livingstone returned to England. It was his first trip home in sixteen years. Imagine the biggest rock star or sports hero you can think of. David Livingstone was even bigger! He was a legend in all of Great Britain. The Royal Geographical Society made a big deal of Livingstone's trek across the African continent. They made him a member of their society. Everywhere Livingstone went, people wanted to say hello or shake his hand. It was believed that only Queen Victoria was more famous.

Livingstone traveled all over the country giving speeches. From his journals, he wrote a book called *Missionary Travels and Researches in South Africa* that became a best seller.

Sales from the book, as well as his prize money from the RGS, meant Livingstone had earned enough money to return to Africa. He sailed from England in March 1858.

MISSIONARY TRAVELS AND RESEARCHES
IN
SOUTH AFRICA.

BY DAVID LIVINGSTONE M D

LONDON
JOHN MURRAY ALBEMARLE STREET

CHAPTER 4
Traveling Man

While David Livingstone was back in South Africa, Henry Morton Stanley was on the move as well. He had moved to Arkansas in 1860. There, he began working as a clerk in a country store, selling everything from guns to candy to curtains.

Arkansas was one of the Southern states that was growing anxious about the question of slavery in the United States. Northern states wanted to abolish slavery, which was more common and widespread in the Southern states, who wanted to leave the United States and form their own country.

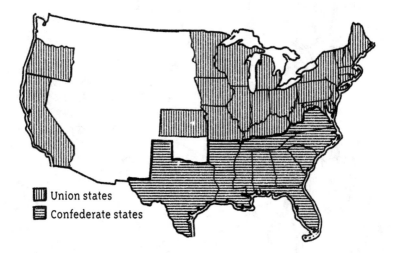

■■ Union states
▤ Confederate states

At first, when the American Civil War officially began in April 1861, twenty-year-old Henry Stanley didn't join in the fighting. After all, he wasn't even an American citizen. But almost everyone else his age was signing up to fight in the war. In June of that year, he joined the Confederate side.

Over the next several months, Stanley marched

hundreds of miles with his fellow soldiers. His feet hurt. He was hot and tired and hungry. The men in his unit ended up in Tennessee to fight in the Battle of Shiloh in April 1862.

The Battle of Shiloh

The American Civil War

The American Civil War was a fight to keep the United States as one nation. It was also a fight to end slavery.

In 1861, the United States was made up of thirty-four states. After Abraham Lincoln was elected president, seven states in the Southern part of the country had decided they no longer wanted to be a part of the

Abraham Lincoln (1809–1865)

United States. They thought that Lincoln's election would bring about an end to their way of life— using enslaved people as free labor—and they also wanted states to have more independent self-rule.

In February 1861, they formed the Confederate States of America and were later joined by four more Southern states. In the eleven Confederate States of America, slavery was still legal. The unpaid labor of enslaved people who were forced to pick the crops (like cotton) made the Southern economy strong.

The Civil War was long and bloody. It is usually estimated that about 620,000 Americans died in the war, although many historians believe the number was much higher. After four years, the Confederacy surrendered to the Union. And in December 1865, the Thirteenth Amendment to the US Constitution officially made slavery illegal in every state.

It was a deadly battle—one of the worst in an awful war. Thousands of men on both sides were killed or wounded at Shiloh. Stanley was taken prisoner by the Union soldiers and sent to Camp Douglas, a prison camp near Chicago, Illinois.

The camp was almost as bad as the war. There were too many men in too small a space, and hundreds died from disease. The Union soldiers figured that Stanley, who was not even a US

Union prison, Camp Douglas

citizen, might be willing to fight for their side if they agreed to release him from the prison camp.

They were right. In June 1862, Stanley switched sides. He joined the Union army and was sent to West Virginia. There, he became sick. While Stanley was in the hospital, his fighting unit moved on without him. Once he recovered, he made his way to Baltimore, Maryland, and boarded a ship back to Liverpool, far away from the American war.

On board, he worked as a deckhand. A deckhand does many different jobs to keep a ship sailing properly. Stanley sailed all over the world: after Liverpool, to Spain, the Caribbean islands, and eventually, back to the United States. There, in 1864, he even joined the US Navy for a year.

Henry Stanley in the US Navy

From a very young age, Henry Morton Stanley could take care of himself. He was willing to try different things and didn't give up easily. He was just twenty-four and already he had lived in several different countries. He had worked as a clerk, a butcher's assistant, a deckhand, and more. He had been in both the US Army and the US Navy.

The *New York Herald* building

And in 1867, Stanley decided he would try his hand at journalism. It turned out he was very good at it! He was able to combine his love of traveling with his ability to tell a great story.

Stanley began his writing career with a newspaper in St. Louis, Missouri. Two years later, he moved to New York City and began writing for the *New York Herald*. It was one of the most-read newspapers in the world at the time.

In his new career, Stanley reported on events all over the world. He traveled to California and in Colorado wrote about the search for gold there. He reported on Native Americans who had been forced to leave their land and their homes in the midwestern United States. He was so good at his job that the *Herald* sent him to work in its office in London. Early in 1869, he wrote about Spain's civil war.

Then in October 1869, the publisher of the *Herald*, James Gordon Bennett Jr., asked Stanley

to report to his office in Paris, France. Stanley was afraid he was about to be fired! Instead, Bennett sent him on the biggest assignment of his life: to find the famous Dr. David Livingstone, who had gone missing in Africa!

James Gordon Bennett Jr.

CHAPTER 5
Lost

When Dr. David Livingstone returned to Africa in 1858, he achieved many more "firsts." He was the first European to see Lake Nyasa (now called Lake Malawi) and to map Lake Chilwa.

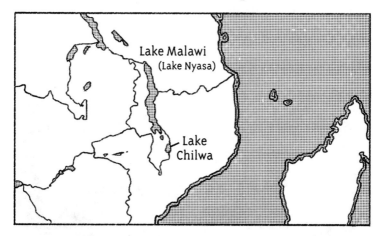

Livingstone had been so successful because he was quite different from other outsiders in Africa. Most European explorers traveled with many people and weapons. To the chief of any local tribe, it could look like an army was coming to take his land and hurt his people. He would be ready, of course, to fight to defend his tribe. However, Livingstone traveled with only enough men to haul supplies. The small group carried only a couple of guns for protection. The local chiefs knew he was a man of peace. As a result, Livingstone had few difficulties with native people as he traveled in Africa.

The local chiefs respected Livingstone because he had taken time to learn their language and customs. He knew how to earn safe passage by being pleasant and giving the tribes something of value to them, such as cloth. Livingstone thought of the men who worked for him as his traveling companions, not his servants.

But Livingstone wasn't perfect. He had a reputation for being stubborn. He usually thought his way was the only way to do things and he didn't always take other people's advice. When things didn't go well, he was not flexible. He wouldn't admit that he was wrong. "I am prepared to go anywhere, provided it be forward," he once famously said.

And when things started to go wrong on this trip, he continued pushing forward. The Zambezi River wasn't navigable after all. The waters were too rough in an area he had not explored before. He tried to follow the path of another river, the Ruvuma, but that failed, too. On this trip, his wife, Mary, had joined him at a camp on the banks of the Zambezi, leaving their children behind in the United Kingdom. She soon caught malaria and never recovered. Mary died in Africa in the spring of 1862. Still, Livingstone moved forward, refusing to accept defeat. He didn't return to England until the summer of 1864.

Grave of Mary Livingstone

When he arrived in London, Livingstone found a debate going on about the source of the famous Nile River in Africa. Some explorers believed it was Lake Victoria. Others felt it was Lake Tanganyika. Who better than the world's most famous explorer to settle the matter?

In 1866, the Royal Geographical Society asked Livingstone to go back to Africa for some answers. They agreed to help pay for the trip. Livingstone jumped at the opportunity. It was a chance for him to make up for what he considered was the failure of the last trip. Plus, he was fifty-three. It might be his last chance to go to Africa.

The Nile River

At more than 4,100 miles long and flowing through ten countries in Africa, the Nile River is usually considered the longest in the world. (Some experts say the Amazon River in South America is longer.) But it is not just a big river. It is the Nile's role in ancient civilization that really makes it so fascinating to historians and explorers.

The Nile was often called the lifeline of ancient Egypt. That's because there is so little rainfall in Egypt that the civilization could not have existed without the water the Nile provided. When the river  overflowed, it left behind rich soil used for growing crops. And the papyrus reeds that grew along the Nile's banks were used for many purposes, including making boats, sandals, baskets, and more.

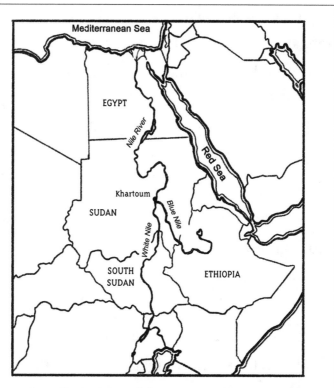

The Nile is formed by two smaller rivers, the Blue Nile and the White Nile. They meet up at Khartoum, the capital city of modern Sudan, and flow north into the Mediterranean Sea. The people of Livingstone's time knew the Mediterranean Sea was where the Nile ended. But they did not know where it began.

Livingstone planned to travel to Lake Tanganyika, a huge freshwater lake in Central Africa, and use a village called Ujiji as his base to find the source of the Nile. Along the way, he explored more areas such as Lake Mweru and Lake Bangweulu.

In April 1867, Livingstone reached Lake Tanganyika. He was very sick. He battled malaria and high fevers. To make matters worse, some of the men who carried Livingstone's supplies—his porters—quit. They took Livingstone's medicine chest with them. He called it the "sorest loss of all. I felt as if now I had received the death sentence."

Livingstone desperately needed medicine. Some of the Arab slave traders were very helpful to him. They carried him to Ujiji. They taught him that boiling his water would cut down on the bacteria that were making him sick. But they refused to deliver any letters for him.

They knew that Livingstone was against the practice of enslaving people and wanted to end their business. So he was left alone.

Livingstone's porters who had quit finally returned to Zanzibar, off the east coast of Africa. They lied about Livingstone and said that he was dead. Most people didn't want to believe the men, but there were no letters—not

one word from the famous doctor.

On April 9, 1868, one year after David Livingstone had reached Lake Tanganyika, the *New York Herald* reported that he seemed to have disappeared. In London, similar stories began appearing almost every week in the newspapers. Where was Dr. Livingstone? Henry Morton Stanley was sent to find out.

CHAPTER 6
Found

James Gordon Bennett Jr., the publisher of the *New York Herald*, believed that finding Livingstone could be the biggest story in the history of his newspaper. Henry Stanley pointed out that it would cost a lot of money to make the trip. But that didn't matter to Bennett. He told Stanley to take as much money as he needed out of the newspaper's bank account to fund the trip. "Draw one thousand pounds now," he told Stanley, "and when you have gone through that, draw another thousand, and when that is spent, draw another thousand, and when you have finished that, draw another thousand, and so on; but FIND LIVINGSTONE!"

Money may not have been a problem,

but Stanley wasn't an explorer. So after Bennett gave him his assignment, Stanley read everything he could about journeying to Africa. He read books by important explorers of the time, such as Richard Francis Burton, John Speke, Edward Daniel Young, and, of course, Dr. David Livingstone.

By the late 1870s, many European nations were interested in establishing settlements—colonies ruled by their own home countries—in Africa. Not only Great Britain, but also Belgium, Germany, France, Italy, Spain, and Portugal all wanted to establish colonies that could profit from the wealth of the silver and gold mines there.

Henry Stanley sailed from New York to Zanzibar, stopping to write a series of travel articles

for the *Herald* along the way. In Zanzibar, he began preparing for his search. He used Bennett's money to hire nearly two hundred porters, who carried cloth, beads, tents, clothes, and materials to make a boat. They brought coffee, tea, sugar, and meat to make meals. They had guns and bullets for protection. And they had plenty of medicine. They had enough supplies and equipment to last for almost two years.

The group was the largest ever to set out exploring from Zanzibar. Stanley and his men set sail for the East African town of Bagamoyo on February 5, 1871, on a ship flying the American flag. On March 21, they began the journey into the interior of Africa to look for Dr. Livingstone. Stanley's goal was Ujiji, about eight hundred miles away. He knew Livingstone wanted to go to Ujiji in his search for the source of the Nile. He also knew it was a main stop for Arab traders. If he didn't find Livingstone at Ujiji, he hoped to at least hear news about him there.

Stanley's route to Ujiji

Stanley was about halfway to Ujiji from Bagamoyo when he wrote his first story for the *Herald* on July 4. Arab traders he met along the way had told him Livingstone was alive. "But wherever he is be sure I shall not give up the chase," he told his readers. "If alive, you shall hear what he has to say. If dead I will find him and bring his bones to you."

Of course, there was no telephone then. Stories such as Stanley's were written and delivered by hand. Stanley gave his reports to traders who were on their way back to Bagamoyo. From there, his stories and letters went by ship to New York. It would be several months before the *Herald* received them.

In the meantime, Stanley slowed down. There was fighting between local tribes that made him take a longer way around to Ujiji. He came down with a severe case of malaria that almost killed him. And there were many quarrels with his porters that could have ended the trip because surely there was no way Stanley could go on without them.

Unlike Livingstone, Stanley was mean to his men to get them to work. Sometimes he even threatened to shoot them! Once, after several

porters ran off in the middle of the night, he sent out a search party the next morning to find them and bring them back in chains.

Still, Stanley moved slowly onward. He traveled through dark jungles, murky swamps, and heavy rains toward Ujiji. He was usually covering no more than four miles per day.

According to Stanley's records, it was early in November 1871 when a caravan of traders coming in the opposite direction told him that there was a white man living in Ujiji.

This man was skinny and frail. His beard was long and bushy. His teeth were gone, and so was his strength. It was hard for him to breathe. He had been sick for so long that he had given up hope—both of finding the source of the Nile and of living very much longer. But who else could it be? No other white man was likely to be within hundreds of miles of the place.

When he was about a mile away, Stanley could see Ujiji. His men raised the American flag. They began firing their guns into the air to celebrate the end of a long journey. It was November 10, 1871. They had walked 975 miles in 236 days.

The villagers rushed out to greet their visitors. A young African man named Susi rushed up to Stanley. "I am the servant of Dr. Livingstone," he said.

Dr. Livingstone! Now there was no doubt. Stanley could barely contain his excitement.

Abdulla Susi

He and his men quickly marched the rest of the way.

Susi rushed into Dr. Livingstone's hut. "An Englishman!" Susi said. "I see him!"

Dr. Livingstone slowly got up from where he was sitting and went outside. He saw the American flag. He saw

dozens of porters carrying loads of supplies. He saw excited villagers gathering around. But he didn't see a white man.

Then Stanley stepped out of the crowd and took off his hat. As he later reported, Stanley said, "Dr. Livingstone, I presume?"

Livingstone had never seen the man before. He didn't know who the visitor was or why he was there. All he knew was that he had been saved. "You have brought me new life," Livingstone said.

After the excitement wore off, the two men went into Livingstone's hut and had a long talk.

They talked about where Livingstone had been and why no one had heard from him in so long. They talked about Lake Tanganyika and looking for the source of the Nile. They talked about nearly everything except exactly who Stanley was and how he had come to be there.

When Stanley admitted the next day that he was a newspaper reporter in search of a story, he was afraid Livingstone might be mad. But the long-lost explorer was just glad to be found.

CHAPTER 7
Together in History

Stanley meant to stay in Ujiji for only a few days. He quickly sent off a message to Zanzibar that he had found Livingstone. Then he figured he would get some rest, hear a few stories from Livingstone, and be on his way. He was in a hurry to get back to New York and share his adventures in the *Herald*. He would give speeches. Maybe he would write a book. Everyone would know him as the man who found David Livingstone!

But after a few days, Henry Stanley wasn't in such a hurry anymore. He started asking Livingstone more and more about exploring. He was learning from the master.

After a few weeks of medicine, food, and

friendship, David Livingstone was feeling much better. He suggested they go exploring together. For the next several months, the two men

traveled into parts of Africa. They paddled about three hundred miles around Lake Tanganyika in a canoe. They marched more than 250 miles to Tabora, another major trading stop.

Stanley asked Livingstone to go back to Zanzibar with him, and from there to England. Livingstone asked Stanley to stay in Africa and keep looking for the source of the Nile with him. Neither man could do what the other wanted, though. And so Livingstone gave Stanley his journals and some letters. They were the proof Stanley needed to show he had found Livingstone.

On March 14, 1872, the two men said goodbye in Tabora. They would never see each other again.

From Tabora, Stanley hiked more than five hundred miles east to Bagamoyo. From there, he sailed first to Zanzibar and then to England.

Livingstone went west back toward Ujiji to continue looking for the source of the Nile River. The world first heard that Stanley had found Livingstone on May 2, 1872, when *The Times* of London reported the news. There just happened to be a British ship in Zanzibar at the time Stanley's message arrived from Ujiji, and its crew heard the news. That ship made it back to London before a separate ship made it back to New York with Stanley's message for the *Herald*. Over the next several days, however, the paper printed story after story about Stanley and Livingstone.

The Source of the Nile

Over 150 years after Stanley found Livingstone, the true source of the Nile River is still not totally settled. Many experts consider Lake Victoria to be its source. But the magic of satellite photography shows that rivers flowing into Lake Victoria provide an even more distant source. One of them is the Kagera River in the hills of Burundi. Still another is in the Nyungwe Forest in Rwanda. Let the debate continue!

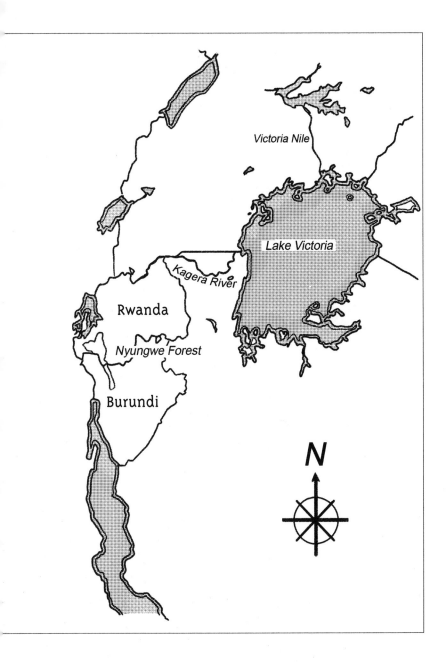

Victoria Nile

Lake Victoria

Kagera River

Rwanda

Nyungwe Forest

Burundi

N

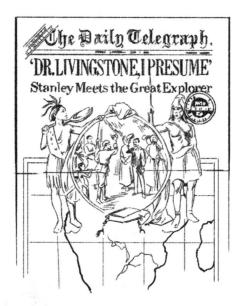

Stanley's famous greeting, "Dr. Livingstone, I presume?" appeared in one of his stories for the *Herald* in the summer of 1872. At first, British newspapers joked about the remark. They couldn't believe Stanley didn't think of something more interesting to say after such a long journey. They were probably just upset, though, that a reporter for an American newspaper was the first to find an explorer who was one of Great Britain's most famous citizens. America was rising in importance in the world, and not everyone in Britain liked that.

Over the years, though, Stanley's greeting to Livingstone has become almost as famous as the explorers themselves. It's been repeated in movies, books, cartoons, and songs. And it's become a standard greeting anytime one person finds someone else they've been looking for.

Stanley left Zanzibar in May 1872 and moved to England. He did indeed write a book about meeting Livingstone. He gave speeches.

He met Queen Victoria. He made a lot of money. And he became famous, too, because he didn't just write about the story, he was also part of it.

Meanwhile, back in Africa, Dr. David Livingstone continued to search for the source of the Nile. But in the spring of 1873, he became very sick again with malaria and dysentery.

He died on May 1, 1873. He was sixty years old.

It was a sad end for Livingstone, mostly because he felt like he had failed at many things. He wanted Africans to believe in Christianity, but few did at that time. He wanted to help put an end to slavery, but it was still going strong when he died. And he wanted to find the source of the Nile, but he didn't.

It wasn't until after his death that many of Livingstone's successes became known. The missions he formed helped generations of Africans get access to education and medical care. His opposition to the slave trade opened the eyes of many to such a horrible practice. And his exploration of Africa helped make it possible for others to follow his clearly mapped routes. Some people who later followed those routes didn't always have the best intentions toward the people already living there. But Livingstone clearly did.

To this day, Livingstone's heart remains in Africa—literally. After his death, Susi and Chuma, two men who were very close to Livingstone, prepared his body for a return to England. They removed his heart and buried it beneath a tree where he died in the village of Chitambo, in present-day Zambia. Then they carried the body more than one thousand miles to Bagamoyo. From there, the British government brought Livingstone to England, where he was buried in famed Westminster Abbey. One of the men who carried his coffin at the funeral was Henry Morton Stanley.

Not long after that, Stanley returned to Africa for nearly three years. He put to good use the knowledge he learned from Livingstone to map the rivers and lakes of Central Africa. He explored all the way around Lake Victoria and Lake Tanganyika, then the length of the Congo River. Unfortunately, as with Livingstone, not everyone used the routes Stanley mapped for the good of

the people living there. Fairly or not, Stanley has sometimes been associated with brutality later inflicted by Europeans on the people in the Congo.

Stanley moved to London and was married to the painter Dorothy Tennant in 1890. In 1895, he was elected to Parliament, the governmental body of Great Britain. In 1899,

Queen Victoria meeting with Stanley

he was knighted by Queen Victoria for services to Britain and became Sir Henry Morton Stanley. He died at age sixty-three on May 10, 1904.

Stanley and Livingstone were two very different people. David Livingstone mostly wanted to change the world. Henry Morton Stanley mostly wanted to be famous.

In the end, Livingstone did change the world—and is famous for it. Stanley became famous—and helped change the world because of it. But they wouldn't have done it without each other.

David Livingstone

Henry Morton Stanley

Timeline of Stanley and Livingstone

1813 — David Livingstone is born in Blantyre, Scotland

1823 — Livingstone begins working in a local cotton mill

1841 — John Rowlands, later Henry Morton Stanley, is born in Denbigh, Wales

— Livingstone arrives in Africa for the first time

1855 — Livingstone names Victoria Falls

1856 — Livingstone returns to England a national hero

1858 — Livingstone begins a six-year expedition in Africa

1862 — Stanley fights in the Battle of Shiloh during the American Civil War

1866 — Livingstone begins his final expedition in Africa to search for the source of the Nile

1869 — Newspaper publisher James Gordon Bennett Jr. asks Stanley to find Livingstone

1871 — Stanley and Livingstone meet in Ujiji on November 10

1872 — On March 14, Stanley and Livingstone part in Africa

1873 — Livingstone dies in Africa on May 1

1874 — Livingstone is buried in Westminster Abbey

1877 — Stanley completes a three-year journey across Africa

1895 — Stanley is elected to Parliament in Great Britain

1904 — Stanley dies in London on May 10

Timeline of the World

1812	The US and Great Britain fight the War of 1812 in North America
1833	The Slavery Abolition Act is passed, to end slavery in most British-owned territories
1848	The California Gold Rush begins
1858	The first communication via transatlantic telegraph cable is sent from Queen Victoria in England to President James Buchanan in the United States
1860	Abraham Lincoln is elected president of the United States
1865	President Lincoln is assassinated in Washington, DC
	The Thirteenth Amendment to the US Constitution officially ends slavery
1876	Alexander Graham Bell receives a patent for his invention, the telephone
1895	German physicist Wilhelm Röntgen discovers X-rays
1899	The British fight the Boer War in South Africa against descendants of Dutch settlers
1903	The Wright brothers fly a plane at Kitty Hawk, North Carolina
	Norwegian explorer Roald Amundsen starts to sail through Canada's Northwest Passage, between the Pacific and Atlantic Oceans

Bibliography

*Books for young readers

Dugard, Martin. *Into Africa: The Epic Adventures of Stanley and Livingstone*. New York: Doubleday, 2003.

Jeal, Tim. *Livingstone*. New York: G.P. Putnam's Sons, 1973.

Jeal, Tim. *Stanley: The Impossible Life of Africa's Greatest Explorer*. New York: Yale University Press, 2007.

*O'Brien, Cynthia. *Explore with Stanley and Livingstone*. Travel with the Great Explorers. New York: Crabtree Publishing Company, 2017.

*Otfinoski, Steven. *David Livingstone: Deep in the Heart of Africa*. Great Explorations. Tarrytown, NY: Marshall Cavendish Benchmark, 2007.

*Stefoff, Rebecca. *Exploration*. World Historical Atlases. Tarrytown, NY: Benchmark Books, 2005.

*St. George, Judith. *So You Want to Be an Explorer?* New York: Philomel Books, 2005.